THE POETRY OF FERMIUM

The Poetry of Fermium

Walter the Educator

Silent King Books

SILENT KING BOOKS

SKB

Copyright © 2024 by Walter the Educator

All rights reserved. No part of this book may be reproduced in any manner whatsoever without written permission except in the case of brief quotations embodied in critical articles and reviews.

First Printing, 2024

Disclaimer
This book is a literary work; poems are not about specific persons, locations, situations, and/or circumstances unless mentioned in a historical context. This book is for entertainment and informational purposes only. The author and publisher offer this information without warranties expressed or implied. No matter the grounds, neither the author nor the publisher will be accountable for any losses, injuries, or other damages caused by the reader's use of this book. The use of this book acknowledges an understanding and acceptance of this disclaimer.

"Earning a degree in chemistry changed my life!"
— Walter the Educator

dedicated to all the chemistry lovers, like myself, across the world

FERMIUM

Born from the fusion of cosmic might,

FERMIUM

In stars' fiery embrace, it took flight,

FERMIUM

A fleeting glimpse in nature's grand design,

FERMIUM

A fleeting moment, yet forever entwined.

FERMIUM

Atomic number one-hundred with grace,

FERMIUM

In laboratories, it finds its space,

FERMIUM

Man's creation, a testament profound,

FERMIUM

To science's conquest, where wonders abound.

FERMIUM

Its nucleus brims with protons galore,

FERMIUM

Neutrons nestled, an atomic core,

FERMIUM

Yet unstable, in flux it resides,

FERMIUM

A testament to where mystery presides.

FERMIUM

Invisible to the naked eye's gaze,

FERMIUM

Its presence felt in the scientist's maze,

FERMIUM

Through careful study and meticulous thought,

FERMIUM

Its secrets unfurl, layer by fraught.

FERMIUM

A fleeting existence, a whispering dream,

FERMIUM

In the realm of atoms, a silent stream,

FERMIUM

Yet in its essence, a story untold,

FERMIUM

Of cosmic journeys, of mysteries bold.

FERMIUM

Its properties, a puzzle to solve,

FERMIUM

In laboratories, where scientists revolve,

FERMIUM

Experimentation, the key to unchain,

FERMIUM

The secrets of Fermium's cryptic domain.

FERMIUM

In the hands of researchers, it transforms,

FERMIUM

Revealing glimpses, in scientific storms,

FERMIUM

Its chemical dance, a complex display,

FERMIUM

In the alchemy of discovery's array.

FERMIUM

With each electron's intricate dance,

FERMIUM

Fermium weaves, in a cosmic trance,

FERMIUM

A symphony of subatomic might,

FERMIUM

In the grand opera of the atomic night.

FERMIUM

Its luminescence, a spectral hue,

FERMIUM

In the darkness of the lab, it imbues,

FERMIUM

A shimmering light, in the void it gleams,

FERMIUM

A beacon of knowledge, in science's schemes.

FERMIUM

From the depths of space, to the scientist's hand,

FERMIUM

Fermium journeys, across the land,

FERMIUM

A symbol of human curiosity,

FERMIUM

In the pursuit of truth's luminosity.

FERMIUM

So let us marvel at Fermium's glow,

FERMIUM

In the world of atoms, where wonders grow,

FERMIUM

For in its mystery, we find our quest,

FERMIUM

To unravel the secrets, of the universe's behest.

ABOUT THE CREATOR

Walter the Educator is one of the pseudonyms for Walter Anderson. Formally educated in Chemistry, Business, and Education, he is an educator, an author, a diverse entrepreneur, and he is the son of a disabled war veteran. "Walter the Educator" shares his time between educating and creating. He holds interests and owns several creative projects that entertain, enlighten, enhance, and educate, hoping to inspire and motivate you.

Follow, find new works, and stay up to date with Walter the Educator™ at WaltertheEducator.com

www.ingramcontent.com/pod-product-compliance
Lightning Source LLC
LaVergne TN
LVHW010619070526
838199LV00063BA/5203